Man:
King of Mind, Body,
And Circumstance

Understanding the Power of Thought
to
Shape Destiny

A Modern Translation
Adapted for the Contemporary Reader

James Allen

Table of Contents

Preface - Message to the Reader

Rebuilding the Greatest Library in Human History

Thousands of years ago, the Library of Alexandria was the heart of global knowledge — a sanctuary where the wisdom of every known civilization was gathered and shared freely.

And then, it was lost.

Now, we're rebuilding it — and you are invited to join us.

At the Library of Alexandria, we've set out to make every book available to *every person on Earth* — not just in print, but in every language, every format, and for every reader.

Here's how we do it:

- **Deluxe Print Editions at True Printing Cost** - Order any book as a high-quality paperback, elegant hardcover, or stunning boxset — and only pay what it costs to print. No markups. No middlemen.
- **Unlimited Access to the Greatest Works** - Enjoy thousands of timeless classics — from Plato to Shakespeare to Tolstoy — in beautiful, modern eBook and audiobook editions. Read and listen without limits — for every reader, everywhere.
- **Modern Translations for Every Language & Dialect** - We're reimagining the classics in clear, accessible language — and translating them into every dialect imaginable. Everyone deserves to understand humanity's greatest ideas.

When you visit **LibraryofAlexandria.com**, you're not just accessing books — you're joining a global movement to restore, preserve, and share the wisdom of civilization.

Join us today at LibraryofAlexandria.com

Together, we'll ensure the light of human wisdom never fades again.

With gratitude,
The Modern Library of Alexandria Team

Visit:

www.libraryofalexandria.com

Or scan the code below:

Introduction

The Sovereign Power Within:
James Allen's Final Testament to Thought
and Destiny

Man – King of Mind represents the culmination of James Allen's lifelong inquiry into the nature of thought, character, and spiritual sovereignty. As one of his final published works, it functions not just as a summary of his key teachings, but as a profound final affirmation: that every person possesses the divine power to shape their destiny through mastery of their own mind. Drawing upon decades of disciplined meditation, philosophical clarity, and ethical reflection, Allen presents a spiritual vision that is both majestic and intensely practical. Here, he speaks not only as a teacher, but as one who has walked the path, suffered its trials, and now stands upon the summit, calling to others to ascend.

This book is not merely motivational—it is revelatory. Allen explores the divine nature of the human mind, emphasizing its capacity for dominion, creativity, and spiritual elevation. Man is not a victim of fate, he insists, but the architect of his own experience.

Thought is the tool, and self-mastery is the key. In Man – King of Mind, Allen reinforces one of his most central ideas: that all outer conditions are the direct result of inner states, and that by governing the mind, one governs life.

This modern edition, Understanding the Power of Thought to Shape Destiny – A Modern Translation – Adapted for the Contemporary Reader, preserves the spiritual intensity and moral rigor of Allen's final teachings while adapting his language to resonate with the clarity and cadence of modern readers. In doing so, it opens a gateway to Allen's highest vision—that each human being is a sovereign power in the universe, and that mastery begins in the secret place of thought.

The Royal Law of Thought: Mind as Creative Force, Destiny as Manifestation

In Man – King of Mind, Allen returns to his central theme with new vigor: the idea that thought shapes reality. He is not content to describe this in metaphorical terms; he insists it is a spiritual law, as exact and consistent as gravity. Just as seeds yield predictable harvests, so do thoughts yield predictable outcomes. When a person habitually thinks with fear, envy, or laziness, their life becomes marked by anxiety, conflict, and stagnation. But when thought is purified—when it is guided by wisdom, love, purpose, and self-control—the outer life becomes an expression of inner truth and peace.

Allen extends this idea beyond personal well-being to touch on the sacred. He sees the mind as the seat of spiritual power, the throne from which we rule our own world. This is not arrogance, but responsibility. The "kingdom" Allen describes is not a domain of others, but of the self: the kingdom of personal destiny, inner experience, and moral influence. To be king of the mind is to reject servitude to impulse, habit, and circumstance—and to choose, with conscious intent, the thoughts that shape one's reality.

Allen's language in this work is more elevated and expansive than in earlier writings. He draws upon imagery of royalty, spiritual law, and divine inheritance. Man, in his view, is not meant to be ruled by fear or external authority, but to awaken the power of disciplined thought and noble purpose. This does not mean denying emotion or human frailty, but transmuting them into strength. Every thought becomes a tool of spiritual construction. Every action becomes the expression of an inner ideal.

This book also emphasizes the importance of spiritual order. Allen teaches that harmony in the outer world reflects harmony in the mind. Disorder, suffering, and injustice arise from internal chaos. Therefore, the first and most urgent work of transformation is not to change society or escape difficulty, but to master one's own mental and moral life. In this framework, self-discipline is not a constraint—it is a coronation. It marks the moment when a person ascends from confusion to command, from drift to direction.

Why Allen's Final Message Still Matters

Man – King of Mind is perhaps James Allen's most comprehensive and spiritually mature work. It distills a lifetime of thought into one unwavering message: you are more powerful than you think, and that power lies in your ability to govern your own mind. In today's culture—so often dominated by distraction, external validation, and victim narratives—Allen's message is a radical and liberating alternative. It reminds us that the path to fulfillment does not begin in the world but within.

What makes this book particularly enduring is its combination of spiritual insight and practical wisdom. Allen's tone is elevated, but never vague. He writes with conviction, but never condemnation. He speaks as a mentor who has tested his principles in the crucible of life and now offers them to others—not as dogma, but as law. His confidence comes not from pride, but from deep inner alignment. His final writings carry a prophetic clarity: a sense that he has seen what lies beyond struggle, and wishes to share the path.

This modern translation seeks to preserve that clarity while making his words accessible to new readers. Allen's original prose is majestic, but at times antiquated. This edition aims to bring the full weight of his message into present-day language, without sacrificing its ethical sharpness or spiritual majesty. It is a book to be read slowly, reflected upon daily, and returned to often.

Ultimately, Man – King of Mind is a call to rise. It is a summons to remember our divine inheritance: the power to choose our thoughts, shape our character, and direct our lives. It challenges us to take the throne within—to become not just thinkers, but creators; not just believers, but builders. May this modern edition serve you as a companion on that noble path, and may it awaken in you the sovereignty that Allen so passionately believed belongs to every soul.

Foreword

The challenge of life is about learning how to live. It's similar to how a schoolboy faces the problem of addition or subtraction. Once he understands it, all the difficulty disappears, and the problem is solved. All the problems in life, whether they are social, political, or religious, come from ignorance and wrong ways of living. As people learn to live correctly and use their strengths, abilities, and minds wisely, the problems of life will be solved. Humanity is currently in the painful process of "learning." It faces the difficulties caused by its own ignorance. As people learn how to live better, how to control their powers and use their abilities with wisdom, the problems of life will be worked out, and the mastery of life will solve the "problems of evil." For the wise, all such problems have already disappeared.

James Allen

> Within, around, above, and below,
> The basic forces burn and wait.
> They wait for wisdom's guiding light;
> In their true form, all things are good:
> Evil exists in their misuse;
> Good comes from their wise and rightful use.

Chapter 1
The Inner World of Thoughts

A person is the creator of both their happiness and misery. Furthermore, they are the ones who continue to create and maintain their own happiness and misery. These things don't come from outside forces; they are conditions that come from within. Their cause is not a god, the devil, or circumstances, but thought. They are the result of actions, and actions are the outward expression of thoughts. A person's fixed state of mind determines their actions, and those actions bring the reactions we call happiness or unhappiness. Because of this, to change the outcome, a person must change their thoughts. To replace misery with happiness, one must reverse the mindset and behavior that cause misery, and happiness will follow. A person can't be happy while thinking and acting selfishly, and they can't be unhappy while thinking and acting unselfishly. Wherever the cause is, the effect will follow. People can't remove the effects, but they can change the causes. They can purify their nature and reshape their character. There is great power in conquering oneself, and great joy in transforming who you are.

Each person is limited by their own thoughts, but they can gradually expand their thinking. They can rise from lower thoughts to higher ones. They can stop holding onto dark and hateful thoughts and instead fill their minds with bright and beautiful ones. As they do this, they will enter a higher world of power and beauty and become aware of a more complete and perfect life.

People live in high or low states depending on the nature of their thoughts. Their world is as dark and small as they believe it to be, or as wide and wonderful as their ability to understand. Everything around them is colored by the thoughts they have.

Think of the person whose mind is suspicious, greedy, and envious. To them, everything seems small, mean, and gloomy. Since they have no greatness within themselves, they can't see greatness anywhere. Being selfish themselves, they can't recognize goodness in others. Even their idea of God is one that can be bribed, and they believe that everyone is as petty and selfish as they are. They see selfish motives behind even the most selfless actions.

Now think of the person whose mind is open, generous, and kind. How wonderful and beautiful their world appears! They see goodness in all creatures and people. They believe people are good, and so they experience goodness from others. In their presence, even the worst people forget their faults and, for a moment, become better. They get a glimpse of a higher way of living, even if just for a short time.

These two types of people, though they may live next door to each other, live in completely different worlds. Their minds are focused on completely different principles. Their actions are opposite. Their understanding of life is totally different. They see two different worlds, and their minds never meet. One is living in misery, the other in happiness, as much as they ever will be. Death won't create a bigger divide between them than the one that already exists. To one, the world is full of thieves. To the other, it's a place filled with goodness. One person keeps a weapon close, always ready to defend against being cheated (not realizing they are really cheating themselves). The other keeps their heart open, always ready to welcome talent, beauty, and goodness. They surround themselves with people of strong character, and these people become part of who they are. They live in a world of thought filled with nobility, and this nobility returns to them many times over in the love and respect of those around them.

The different levels of society are nothing more than different states of thought, expressed through behavior. Someone may complain about these divisions, but they can't change or affect them. There is no quick fix to equalize people who think differently, as they are separated by the fundamental principles of life. The lawless and the law-abiding will always be apart, and it's not hate or pride that separates them, but differences in understanding and behavior that don't connect. Those who are rude and poorly mannered are kept out of the circles of the gentle and refined by the mental barrier of their own behavior, which they can only remove through self-improvement. They can't force their way into a better life through violence or rudeness. The path to better living comes by following its principles. A rough person will always find themselves among others like them, while a kind person will find themselves among a community of the good. Everyone reflects their surroundings, showing the world the state of their own mind. Each person looks at the world and sees a reflection of themselves.

Everyone moves within the limits of their own thoughts. Anything beyond those thoughts doesn't exist to them. People only know what they've grown to understand. The smaller their thinking, the more convinced they are that nothing else exists. They can't understand bigger minds or greater ideas because they haven't grown to that point yet. A person with a broad way of thinking understands the smaller ways of thinking they've already outgrown. In the greater experience of life, all smaller experiences are included. When their thinking grows to include wisdom, they will realize there are even wider ways of thinking and living that they don't yet fully understand.

Just like schoolchildren, people find themselves in different stages of life based on their knowledge or ignorance. A younger student doesn't understand the lessons of an advanced class, but they will reach it through effort and growth. By learning everything in between, they eventually reach the highest level. Beyond that is the teacher's understanding. In life, people who live selfishly and chase personal desires can't understand those who live unselfishly and think deeply, but they can reach that higher level through effort, right actions, and growth in moral understanding. Above all these levels are the great Teachers of humanity, the Masters and Saviors of the world, whom followers of different religions worship. Just like students, there are levels of teachers. Some have not yet reached the highest rank of Master but are still guides and teachers due to their strong moral character. Just holding a position of authority doesn't make someone a true teacher. A true teacher is someone who earns the respect and admiration of others through their moral greatness.

Each person is as low or high, small or great, as bad or noble as their thoughts. Nothing more, nothing less. Each person moves within the world of their own thoughts, and that world becomes their reality. In the world they create through their thinking, they find the people and experiences that match their growth. But no one has to stay in the lower worlds. They can lift their thoughts and rise higher. They can move beyond their current situation into higher levels of life and happiness. Whenever they choose, they can break free from selfish thinking and breathe the pure air of a greater life.

Chapter 2
The Outer World of Things

The world around us is connected to the world of thoughts. The inner world shapes the outer one. The bigger picture holds the smaller one. Matter is connected to the mind. Events are streams of thought, and circumstances are combinations of thought. The external conditions and actions of others that a person is involved in are closely related to their own mental needs and development. A person is a part of their surroundings. They aren't separate from others but are tied to them through actions and by the laws of thought, which form the foundation of human society.

You can't change the outside world to fit your passing desires, but you can set aside your desires. You can change your attitude towards the outside world, and it will start to look different. You can't control the actions of others, but you can control your own actions toward them. You can't break through the walls of circumstance that surround you, but you can adapt to them or find your way to bigger opportunities by expanding your mind. Things follow thoughts. Change your thoughts, and your circumstances will change too. To reflect clearly, a mirror must be smooth. A distorted mirror gives back a distorted image, and a troubled mind sees the world in a distorted way. Calm your mind, organize it, and bring it peace, and you'll see a more beautiful reflection of the world, a clearer understanding of life.

A person has all the power within their own mind to purify and perfect it, but their power over the outer world and other people is limited. This becomes clear when we realize that everyone is just one individual among many, each one connected to others. People don't act independently; they respond to and interact with each other. What you do affects others, and they will respond to your actions. If your actions harm them, they will defend themselves. Just as the human body removes harmful cells, society pushes out harmful members. Your wrong actions are like wounds on society, and healing those wounds will bring you pain and sorrow. This cause-and-effect relationship in ethics is no different from the one we see in physical life. It's just a broader application of the same law. No action is separate from others. Your most private deed is recorded in some way—it brings joy if it's good and pain if it's bad. There's truth in the old story of "the Book of Life," where every thought and action is written down and judged. This is because your actions belong not just to you but to humanity and the universe. You can't stop the effects of external events, but you have all the power to change and correct the internal causes. This makes improving your own actions your highest duty and greatest achievement.

The flip side of this truth— that you can't stop external events— is that external events can't harm you. Your bondage or your freedom comes from within. The harm that comes to you from others is just the result of your own actions and mindset. Others are simply the instruments; you are the cause. Destiny is the result of your actions. Every person gets what they deserve, whether good or bad. The righteous person is free. No one can harm them, destroy them, or take away their peace. Their understanding of life protects them from being hurt by others. Any harm that others try to cause them ends up hurting those others instead, leaving the righteous person unharmed. The good that flows from them is their endless source of happiness and strength. Its root is peace, and its flower is joy.

The harm someone sees in the actions of another— like an insult— isn't in the action itself, but in their attitude toward it. The hurt and unhappiness come from within. The person mistakenly believes that the insult can damage their character, but it has no such power. The only one harmed by the act is the person who did it. By believing they've been hurt, the person becomes upset and restless, trying to counter the supposed harm. But these actions only make the insult seem more real and give it more power. All their stress and unhappiness come from how they received the insult, not from the insult itself. A righteous person has proven this by staying calm and unaffected in the same situation. They understand it and therefore ignore it. It belongs to a mindset they've outgrown and no longer connect with. They don't take the insult personally because the thought of being hurt doesn't cross their mind. They live above the mental chaos where such actions thrive, and these actions can no more harm them than a child throwing stones can harm the sun. Buddha often told his followers that as long as someone can still think, "I've been hurt," or "I've been cheated," or "I've been insulted," they haven't understood the truth.

The same is true for external things like circumstances and surroundings. They aren't good or bad in themselves; it's our attitude and mindset that make them seem that way. A person might think they could do great things if only they weren't held back by their circumstances—lack of money, time, influence, or freedom from family responsibilities. But in reality, these things aren't holding them back. They are giving these circumstances a power they don't actually have and are giving in to their own weaknesses. The real thing holding them back is their lack of the right mindset. When they start seeing their circumstances as challenges that help them grow, when they realize that what they see as "obstacles" are actually the steps they need to take to achieve their goals, then their needs will lead to new ideas, and the obstacles will turn into opportunities. The person is the key factor. If their mind is healthy and focused, they won't complain about their circumstances but will rise above them. A person who complains about their circumstances hasn't yet grown into full maturity, and life will keep challenging them until they grow strong enough to overcome those challenges. Circumstances are harsh for the weak but obedient to the strong.

It's not external things that bind us or set us free; it's our thoughts about them. We create our own chains and build our own prisons, or we set ourselves free and build our own palaces. If I think my surroundings are holding me back, that thought will keep me trapped. If I believe that my thoughts and actions can rise above my surroundings, that belief will set me free. We should ask ourselves, "Are my thoughts leading me to freedom or keeping me trapped?" We should let go of the thoughts that bind us and adopt those that set us free.

If we fear other people's opinions, poverty, the loss of friends or influence, then we are truly bound and cannot know the inner happiness of the enlightened, the freedom of the just. But if our thoughts are pure and free, if we see the challenges and changes in life as opportunities for growth rather than reasons for fear, then nothing can stop us from achieving our goals, for then we are truly free.

Chapter 3
Habit: Its Slavery and Its Freedom

Man is subject to the law of habit. Does that mean he's not free? No, he is free. Man didn't create life or its laws; they are eternal. He finds himself living under them, and he can understand and follow them. Man's power doesn't lie in making the laws of life; it lies in his ability to choose and make decisions. Man doesn't create any of the universal laws or conditions; they are the fundamental principles of existence, and they can't be made or undone. He discovers them; he doesn't create them. Ignoring them is the root of the world's suffering. Defying them is foolish and leads to enslavement. Who is freer—the thief who breaks the laws of his country, or the honest citizen who obeys them? Who is freer—the fool who thinks he can live however he wants, or the wise person who chooses to do what is right?

By nature, man is a creature of habit, and that can't be changed. But he can change his habits. He can't change the law of his nature, but he can adapt himself to it. No one tries to change the law of gravity, but everyone adapts to it. We use it by working with it, not by defying or ignoring it. People don't run into walls or jump off cliffs hoping the law will change for them. They walk along walls and avoid cliffs.

Man can't escape the law of habit any more than he can escape the law of gravity, but he can use it wisely or foolishly. Just as scientists and inventors master physical forces by obeying and using them, wise people master spiritual forces in the same way. While the bad man is a slave to his habits, the good man is their wise director and master. He's not the creator of the law of habit, nor its dictator, but he controls it through knowledge and self-discipline. A bad man has bad habits of thought and action. A good man has good habits of thought and action. The bad man becomes good by changing his habits. He doesn't change the law; he changes himself and adapts to the law. Instead of giving in to selfish desires, he follows moral principles. He becomes the master of the lower by serving the higher. The law of habit remains the same, but he changes from bad to good by readjusting himself to the law.

Habit is repetition. Man repeats the same thoughts, actions, and experiences over and over again until they become part of him and are built into his character. Skill is a fixed habit. Growth is mental accumulation. Today, man is the result of millions of repeated thoughts and actions. He isn't born complete; he becomes, and is always becoming. His character is determined by his own choices. The thoughts and actions he chooses become part of him through habit.

Each person is an accumulation of their thoughts and actions. The traits they show automatically are the result of long repetition, making their behavior instinctive. Habit eventually becomes unconscious, repeating itself without the person making a choice or effort. Over time, it takes full control of a person, making it seem like their will is powerless to resist it. This happens with all habits, whether good or bad. When bad, we say the person is a "victim" of a bad habit or has a vicious mind. When good, we say they have a "good disposition" by nature.

Everyone is subject to their habits, whether they are good or bad—that is, to their repeated and accumulated thoughts and actions. Knowing this, a wise person chooses to form good habits because this kind of submission brings joy, peace, and freedom. On the other hand, giving in to bad habits leads to misery, wretchedness, and slavery.

This law of habit is good because, while it allows a person to chain themselves to bad behaviors, it also allows them to become so fixed in good behaviors that they do them automatically, without struggle or effort, and in complete happiness and freedom. Seeing how automatic life can become, some people have denied that humans have willpower or freedom. They say that people are "born" good or bad and that they are helpless tools of blind forces.

It's true that people are the result of mental forces—in fact, they are those forces—but they are not blind. People can direct and redirect them. In other words, people can take control of themselves and change their habits. It's also true that a person is born with a certain character, but that character is the result of countless lives in which it was slowly built through choice and effort. In this life, it will be shaped by new experiences.

No matter how trapped a person seems by a bad habit or character trait—and both are the same—they can free themselves, as long as they are sane. They can replace the bad habit with a good one, and when the good habit becomes as strong as the bad one was, they will feel constant happiness instead of constant misery.

Whatever a person has created within themselves, they can break apart and recreate whenever they wish. A person won't want to get rid of a bad habit as long as they find it enjoyable. But when it becomes painful and controlling, they will start looking for a way out and eventually replace the bad with something better.

No one is helplessly trapped. The same law that made them a slave to bad habits will allow them to become the master of themselves. All they have to do is act on this truth—deliberately stop following old ways of thinking and behaving, and work hard to create new and better ones. It may take more than a day, a week, a month, a year, or even five years, but this shouldn't discourage them. Time is needed for the new habits to take hold and the old ones to break down. But the law of habit is certain, and effort that is steady and never abandoned will always lead to success. If a bad habit, which is a negative condition, can become strong and permanent, how much more can a good habit, which is a positive force, become strong and powerful! A person is only powerless to overcome bad habits as long as they think they are powerless. If a bad habit is combined with the thought, "I can't change," the bad habit will stay. Nothing can be overcome until the thought of powerlessness is removed and destroyed. The real obstacle isn't the habit itself, but the belief that it can't be overcome. How can a person break a bad habit if they're convinced it's impossible? How can they be stopped from overcoming it when they know they can and are determined to do it? The main thought that enslaves people is the idea, "I can't overcome my weaknesses." When we bring this thought out into the open, it becomes clear that it's just a belief in the power of evil, and a lack of belief in the power of good. For a person to say or believe they can't rise above wrong thinking and wrong behavior is to submit to evil and give up on good.

Through these kinds of thoughts, people trap themselves. Through the opposite thoughts, they set themselves free. A change in attitude changes character, habits, and life. Man is his own liberator. He has created his own chains, and he can break free from them. Throughout history, people have looked for an external savior, but they remain trapped. The true liberator is within. It is the Spirit of Truth, and the Spirit of Truth is the Spirit of Good. Those who live in good thoughts and actions live in the Spirit of Good.

Man isn't trapped by any power outside of his own wrong thoughts, and he can free himself from them. The thoughts that enslave him the most are: "I can't rise," "I can't break my bad habits," "I can't change my nature," "I can't control myself," and "I can't stop sinning." None of these "can'ts" exist in the things they refer to; they only exist in the person's thoughts.

These negative thoughts are bad habits of thinking that need to be removed. In their place, we must plant the positive thought, "I can," and nurture it until it becomes a strong habit, bearing the fruit of right and happy living.

Habit binds us, and habit sets us free. Habit starts in thought, then shows in action. Change your thoughts from bad to good, and your actions will follow. Stick with bad thoughts, and they will bind you tighter. Stick with good thoughts, and they will lead you to greater freedom. If someone loves their chains, let them stay bound. But if someone thirsts for freedom, let them come and be set free.

Chapter 4
Bodily Conditions

Today, there are many schools focused on healing the body, which shows how common physical suffering is. Just as the numerous religions show how widespread mental suffering is. Each of these healing methods has its place as long as it can relieve pain, even if it doesn't completely eliminate the problem. Despite all these schools of healing, disease and pain remain, just as sin and sorrow still exist despite the many religions.

Disease and pain, like sin and sorrow, are too deeply rooted to be cured with temporary fixes. Our problems have ethical causes deeply rooted in the mind. This doesn't mean physical conditions have no role in illness—they are important as instruments or parts of the chain of cause and effect. For example, the microbe that caused the Black Death was a result of uncleanliness, and uncleanliness is, at its core, a moral disorder. Matter is the physical expression of the mind, and the physical struggle we call disease has a connection to the mental struggle linked to sin. In his current self-aware state, man's mind is often disturbed by conflicting desires, and his body is attacked by unhealthy elements. He is out of balance mentally and physically. Animals in their wild state are free from disease because they live in harmony with their surroundings. They have no moral responsibilities or sense of sin, and they don't experience the emotional turmoil of guilt, grief, or disappointment that disrupts human harmony and happiness. Their bodies are not affected by these disturbances. As man rises to a higher, divine state of consciousness, he will leave behind all these inner conflicts, overcome sin and the sense of sin, and get rid of guilt and sorrow. By restoring mental harmony, he will also restore physical harmony and health.

The body is a reflection of the mind, and it shows the visible signs of hidden thoughts. The outer world follows the inner world, and in the future, enlightened scientists may be able to trace every physical illness back to its ethical cause in the mind.

Mental harmony, or moral wholeness, leads to physical health. It doesn't create it instantly, as if someone took a pill and became healthy, but if the mind becomes more balanced and calm, if the person grows morally, then a solid foundation for physical health is being built. The body's energy will be better directed, and even if perfect health isn't achieved, any physical disorder will lose its power to overwhelm the stronger, uplifted mind.

Someone who suffers physically won't necessarily be cured right away when they start living according to moral and harmonious principles. In fact, for a while, as the body goes through changes and sheds the effects of past imbalances, the illness may seem to get worse. Just as a person doesn't gain perfect peace the moment they start living righteously—except in rare cases—they also don't instantly achieve perfect health. Both mental and physical adjustment take time, and even if perfect health isn't reached, it can still be improved.

When the mind is strong, the body becomes less important and stops being the main focus it is for many people. If a sickness isn't cured, the mind can rise above it and refuse to be controlled by it. One can be happy, strong, and useful even with a physical illness. The common claim made by health experts that a happy, successful life is impossible without physical health is disproved by the fact that many people who have accomplished great things—people of genius and exceptional talent—have suffered from physical ailments. There are many living examples of this today. Sometimes, a physical illness even stimulates mental activity and helps rather than hinders.

Making a happy, useful life depend on health puts the body before the mind and makes the spirit serve the body. People with strong minds don't focus on their physical condition if it's not perfect—they ignore it and continue to work and live as if it weren't there. Ignoring the body keeps the mind sane and strong, and it's also one of the best ways to heal the body. If we can't have a perfectly healthy body, we can have a healthy mind, and a healthy mind is the best path to a healthy body.

A weak mind is worse than a sick body, and it often leads to physical illness. A mental invalid is in a much worse state than a physical invalid. There are people (every doctor knows them) who only need to lift themselves into a strong, happy state of mind to realize that their bodies are healthy and capable.

Weak thoughts about oneself, one's body, and food should be let go of by anyone who wants to live fully. Someone who believes that the healthy food they're eating is going to hurt them needs to regain physical strength through mental strength. Thinking that your health and safety depend on a specific kind of food, which isn't found in most homes, leads to small, unnecessary problems. A vegetarian who avoids potatoes, believes fruit causes indigestion, apples give acidity, pulses are poison, or fears green vegetables, is making their beliefs seem foolish to those robust meat eaters who don't have such fears and self-obsession. Believing that the simple, natural foods of the earth, eaten when you're hungry, are harmful shows a complete misunderstanding of the purpose of food. Food is meant to sustain and preserve the body, not harm it. It's a strange belief—and one that harms the body—that leads so many people who are focused on diet to think that certain pure, natural foods are bad. I once spoke with someone who believed that their illness (and the illnesses of thousands of others) was caused by eating bread—not by eating too much bread, but by the bread itself. And yet, this person's bread was homemade, whole-grain bread. Before blaming our diseases on such innocent things, we should get rid of our sins, weak thoughts, self-indulgence, and foolish excesses.

Focusing on our minor troubles and illnesses is a sign of weak character. Dwelling on them leads to talking about them more, which makes them even more vivid in the mind, soon weakening the mind through all this pity and attention. It's just as easy to focus on happiness and health as on misery and illness. It's just as easy to talk about them, and much more pleasant and useful to do so.

"Let us live happily, without hating those who hate us! Among those who hate us, let us live without hatred! Let us live happily, free from sickness among the sick! Among the sick, let us live free from sickness! Let us live happily, free from greed among the greedy! Among the greedy, let us live free from greed!"

Moral principles are the best foundation for health and happiness. They guide behavior and cover every aspect of life. When they are truly understood and embraced, they force a person to reorganize their entire life, down to the smallest details. While guiding someone's diet, they eliminate food fears, pickiness, and unfounded ideas about the dangers of certain foods. When sound moral health removes self-indulgence and self-pity, all natural foods will be seen for what they are—nourishment for the body, not its enemy.

So, when we think about physical conditions, we are always brought back to the mind and the moral virtues that protect it. The morally strong are physically strong. Constantly changing your behavior based on passing thoughts and feelings, without following solid principles, leads to confusion. But disciplining your actions through moral principles allows you to see everything in its proper place.

Only moral principles have the ability to see moral order in life. They give the insight to see the causes of things and the power to command all details to fall into place, like a magnet attracting steel filings.

Better than curing the body is rising above it—being its master, not letting it control you. Don't abuse the body or give in to it, and don't let its needs come before virtue. Discipline its pleasures and don't be defeated by its pains. In short, live in the balance and strength of moral power. This, better than a physical cure, is a reliable way to cure the body, and it is a constant source of mental strength and spiritual peace.

Chapter 5
Poverty

Throughout history, many of the greatest men have given up wealth and chosen poverty so they could better accomplish their noble goals. So why is poverty seen as such a terrible thing? Why is this poverty, which these great men considered a blessing and embraced like a bride, viewed by most people as something to fear and avoid? The answer is simple. In the case of these great men, poverty is linked to a noble mind that not only removes all appearance of evil but also elevates poverty, making it seem good and beautiful. It becomes so attractive and desirable that, seeing the dignity and happiness of the noble beggar, many others follow their example by choosing the same lifestyle. But in the other case, the poverty of our big cities is connected to everything mean and ugly—swearing, drunkenness, filth, laziness, dishonesty, and crime. So what is the real evil—is it poverty, or is it sin? The answer is clear—it is sin. Take sin away from poverty, and the sting is gone. Poverty no longer seems like a terrible evil and can even be turned to good and noble purposes. Confucius praised one of his poor students, named Yen-hwui, as an example of high virtue to his wealthier students.

Even though Yen-hwui was so poor he had to live on rice and water and had no better shelter than a small hut, he never complained. Where this poverty would have made others discontented and miserable, it didn't disturb his peace. Poverty cannot harm a noble character, but it can highlight it. Yen-hwui's virtues shone even brighter because of his poverty, like jewels standing out against a contrasting background.

Many social reformers tend to see poverty as the cause of the sins connected to it, yet these same reformers say that the immoral actions of the rich are caused by their wealth. Where there is a cause, the effect will follow. If wealth caused immorality and poverty caused degradation, then every rich person would be immoral, and every poor person would be degraded.

An evil person will do wrong in any situation, whether they are rich, poor, or somewhere in between. A good person will do what's right no matter what. Extreme circumstances may bring out the evil that is already there, waiting for a chance to show itself, but they don't cause the evil or create it.

Being discontent with your financial situation is not the same as being poor. Many people think they're poor even though they earn hundreds or even thousands of pounds a year and have few responsibilities. They believe they're suffering from poverty, but their real problem is greed. They aren't unhappy because they're poor but because they want more wealth. Poverty is often in the mind more than in the wallet. As long as a man thirsts for more money, he will feel poor, and in that sense, he is poor because greed is poverty of the mind. A miser may be a millionaire, but he is as poor as he was when he had no money.

On the other hand, the problem with many people living in poverty and degradation is that they are satisfied with their condition. To live in filth, laziness, and selfish indulgence, surrounded by foul thoughts, foul language, and dirty surroundings, and still be content with oneself, is sad. Here again, "poverty" is really a mental condition, and the solution to this "problem" lies in improving the individual from the inside, not just changing their outer situation. When a man becomes clean and alert inside, he will no longer be content with filth and degradation outside. Once his mind is in order, he will put his house in order too. In fact, both he and others will know that he has changed on the inside because he will have changed his immediate surroundings as well. His transformed heart will be seen in his transformed life.

Of course, there are people who are neither deceiving themselves nor degrading themselves, yet they are still poor. Many of these people are content to remain poor. They are happy, hardworking, and satisfied, and they don't want anything else. But for those among them who are not content and want better surroundings and more opportunities, they should—and usually do—use their poverty as a motivator to work harder and develop their skills. Through self-improvement and dedication to their responsibilities, they can rise to the fuller, more responsible life they desire.

Devotion to duty is not only the way out of poverty when it is seen as limiting; it is also the best path to wealth, influence, lasting happiness, and even perfection. When understood deeply, it is connected to everything that is best and noblest in life. It includes energy, hard work, focused attention on the work of one's life, single-minded purpose, courage, faithfulness, determination, self-reliance, and the self-discipline that is the key to true greatness. A very successful man was once asked, "What's the secret of your success?" He replied, "Getting up at six o'clock in the morning and minding my own business." Success, honor, and influence always come to the person who diligently attends to their own responsibilities and avoids interfering with the duties of others.

Some may argue, as is often the case, that most people in poverty—like mill and factory workers—don't have the time or opportunity to pursue any special work. This is not true. Time and opportunity are always available to everyone at all times. Those poor workers who are content to stay where they are can always be diligent in their factory work and find happiness and sobriety in their homes. But those who feel they are capable of more can prepare for it by educating themselves in their spare time. The hard-working poor are the ones who most need to save their time and energy. A young person who wants to escape poverty must start by giving up the foolish and wasteful habits of drinking alcohol, smoking, sexual immorality, late nights at clubs and parties, and must devote their evenings to improving their mind through education, which is necessary for their progress. This is how many of the most influential people in history—including some of the greatest—raised themselves from the deepest poverty. This fact proves that necessity is the best opportunity, not, as is often claimed, the end of opportunity. The deeper the poverty, the greater the motivation to act for those who are dissatisfied with themselves and determined to achieve something.

Poverty is either a good or a bad thing depending on the character and mindset of the person experiencing it. Wealth is the same way. Tolstoy felt trapped by his wealth. To him, it was a great burden. He longed for poverty the way greedy people long for wealth. However, vice is always an evil because it degrades the individual who engages in it and is a danger to society. A serious and thoughtful study of poverty always leads back to the individual and the human heart. When social reformers condemn vice as strongly as they condemn wealth, and when they are as eager to end wrong living as they are to raise wages, we will start to see a reduction in the degraded kind of poverty that is one of the darkest parts of our society. Before that type of poverty disappears entirely, the human heart will need to go through a radical transformation during the process of evolution. When the heart is cleansed of greed and selfishness, when drunkenness, impurity, laziness, and self-indulgence are banished from the earth, then poverty and riches will be no more. Every person will do their work with a deep joy that is still unknown to most people today. Everyone will eat the fruit of their labor with self-respect and in perfect peace.

Chapter 6
Man's Spiritual Dominion

The kingdom that man is meant to rule over with complete control is his own mind and life. But this kingdom isn't separate from the rest of the world—it's connected to all of humanity, to nature, to the events he is involved in, and to the vast universe. So, mastering this kingdom includes mastering the knowledge of life itself. It lifts a man to the height of wisdom, giving him insight into people's hearts, the ability to tell the difference between good and evil, and even understand what goes beyond both good and evil. It also gives him the ability to see the true nature of actions and their consequences.

Right now, people are under the control of rebellious thoughts, and conquering these is the greatest victory in life. Those who are unwise think that they can master everything but themselves, and they try to find happiness for themselves and others by changing things on the outside. But changing outer circumstances can't bring lasting happiness or wisdom. Trying to fix a body burdened by sin won't bring health and well-being. The wise understand that true mastery only comes when the self is conquered, and when a person gains control over themselves, they naturally gain control over the things around them. These wise people find happiness always rising up from within, in the calm strength of divine virtue. They let go of sin, and they purify and strengthen their bodies by rising above the control of their desires.

Man can rule over his own mind and be the master of himself. Until he does, his life will feel incomplete and unsatisfactory. His spiritual power comes from mastering the mental forces that make up his nature. The body doesn't have the power to cause anything. Ruling the body—meaning appetite and passion—is really about disciplining the mental forces behind them. Subduing, changing, redirecting, and transforming the conflicting spiritual forces inside is the great and powerful work that everyone must eventually do. For a long time, man sees himself as a slave to outside forces, but there comes a day when his spiritual eyes open, and he realizes that all along, he has been a slave only to his own uncontrolled, unpurified self. On that day, he rises up and takes his place on his spiritual throne. He no longer follows his desires, appetites, and passions like a slave, but from then on, he rules them like subjects. The mental world he used to wander through like a helpless beggar or a beaten servant, he now discovers is his by right of self-control. It's his to organize and bring into harmony, to stop its conflicts and contradictions, and to bring it to a place of peace.

By rising up and using his rightful spiritual authority, he joins the ranks of the great ones who, throughout all of history, have conquered and achieved. These are the people who have overcome ignorance, darkness, and mental suffering and have risen into the light of Truth.

Chapter 7
Conquest: Not Resignation

Anyone who has taken on the great task of overcoming themselves does not give in to anything that is evil. They only surrender to what is good. Giving up to evil is the lowest form of weakness, but obeying what is good is the highest form of strength. To give up to sin, sorrow, ignorance, and suffering is like saying, "I give up; I am defeated; life is evil, and I accept it." Such surrender to evil is the opposite of true religion. It's a direct rejection of good, placing evil in the position of ultimate power in the universe. This kind of submission leads to a selfish and sad life, a life without the strength to resist temptation or the joy and peace that come from a mind ruled by good.

Man is not meant to live in constant defeat and sorrow, but for final victory and happiness. All the spiritual laws of the universe support the good man, because good preserves and protects. Evil has no laws—it only destroys and causes harm.

Right now, changing our character from evil to good is not a part of normal education. Even many religious teachers have lost this knowledge and practice, so they can't teach it. For most people, moral growth happens unconsciously, as they deal with the challenges of life. But the time will come when consciously building character will be a key part of teaching young people. No one will be allowed to be a preacher unless they are someone who practices self-control, has perfect honesty, and lives a pure life. This way, they will be able to teach others how to build their character, which will become the main focus of religion.

The teaching presented here is about conquering evil, getting rid of sin, and establishing man in the knowledge of good and the experience of lasting peace. This is the teaching of the great spiritual leaders throughout all ages. No matter how much this teaching may have been misunderstood or misrepresented by those who are not enlightened, it is the teaching of all the perfect ones of the past and will be the teaching of all the perfect ones to come. It is the teaching of Truth.

This conquest is not about defeating some external evil—not about overcoming evil people, evil spirits, or evil things. It's about conquering the evil within—our own evil thoughts, desires, and actions. For when each person has destroyed the evil within their own heart, where in the entire universe will anyone be able to point and say, "There is evil"? On that great day when all people are good within, all traces of evil will disappear from the world. Sin and sorrow will no longer exist, and there will be everlasting joy for all.

Thank you for Reading

You've Just Read a Piece of the Greatest Library Ever Rebuilt

Thank you for reading.

This book is one of thousands we're restoring, reimagining, and translating as part of the **Modern Library of Alexandria** — a global movement to preserve and share humanity's most important ideas.

What was once lost to fire and time is now rising again — not just as memory, but as living, breathing knowledge, freely accessible to all.

What You Can Do Next:

- **Keep Reading.**

    Discover more legendary works — in beautiful print, audiobook, or digital form — at LibraryofAlexandria.com.

- **Build Your Own Library.**

    Every title is available as a paperback, hardcover, or collectible boxset — at true printing cost. Craft a personal library worthy of display.

- **Spread the Light.**

    Share this book. Tell others about the movement. Help us translate every timeless work into every language, so no reader is ever left behind.

By finishing this book, you've already taken part in something extraordinary.

Join us at LibraryofAlexandria.com

Together, we're rebuilding the greatest library the world has ever known.

With appreciation,
The Modern Library of Alexandria Team

Visit:

www.libraryofalexandria.com

Or scan the code below: